DID YOU KNOW that there are special
powers inside every one of us?

Finding mine took a long time.
But when I found them, everything changed!

It all started when I learned the true
meaning of my name.

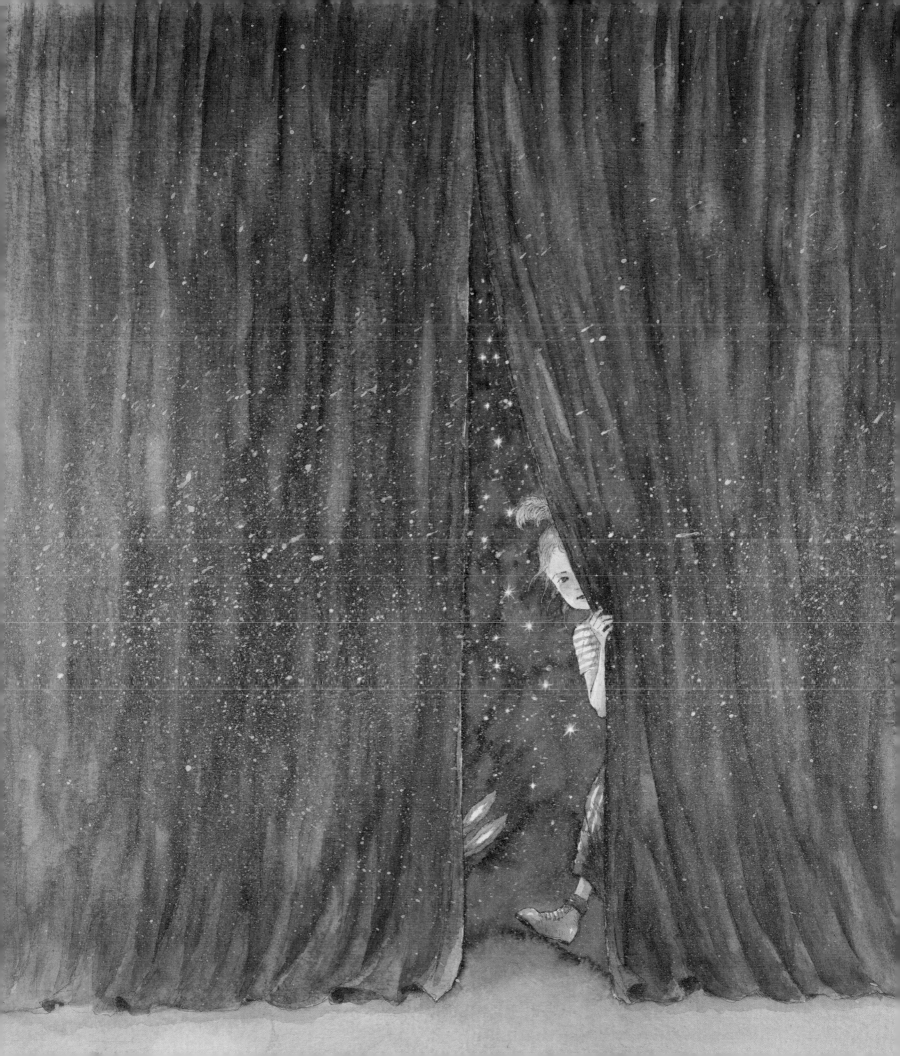

To my daughter, to new beginnings,
and to finding the power that lies within all of us.

—D. K.

For Luc

—C.U.

Text copyright © 2022 by Diane Kruger
Illustrations copyright © 2022 by Christa Unzner

MINEDITIONUS
An imprint of Astra Books for Young Readers,
a division of Astra Publishing House
astrapublishinghouse.com
Printed in China
ISBN: 978-1-6626-5091-8 (hc)
ISBN: 978-1-6626-5092-5 (eBook)
Library of Congress Control Number: 2022904560

First edition

10 9 8 7 6 5 4 3 2 1

This book was illustrated in watercolor and typeset in EideticModern.
Design by Amelia Mack

Diane Kruger

A Name from the Sky

ILLUSTRATED BY
Christa Unzner

MINEDITIONUS

IN THE SMALL village in Germany where I grew up, all the other children thought I was strange.

I didn't like playing soccer or catch.
And my pet bunny, whose name was Benny,
came everywhere with me.

My best friends were the characters in my books. I loved telling Benny all about them.

Benny and I loved reading about faraway places
and people from other lands.

I also liked dancing all by myself, in the forest behind my house.

There was something else that made me stick out.
My name.

Diane

No one in my village had ever heard of such a name!
It didn't sound German at all, like Anna or Lena or Heidi.
Why did I have to be Diane?

But then one day, my mom showed me a book
about a powerful goddess.

"You see, Diane, you are named after her," Mom said.

"Your name comes from the sky, and from the forest.
When the moon was full, she dashed through the
woods with her bow and quiver."

Mom told me even more about the goddess.
"She was a fearless huntress, strong-willed, with
magical powers. She brought light and kindness
wherever she went. And just like you, she loved the
forest and looked after the animals."

"One day, my love, you will learn to use your own given powers," Mom said. "You'll travel the world, and people will see how well your name matches the woman you have become."

I couldn't believe what I was hearing: Me?
As special as a goddess?
What could my powers possibly be?

I started going to the forest behind our house every
night, hoping to see her. While I was waiting, I told
Benny all about the adventures I would have and the
places I would visit once I found my powers. Oh, how
we laughed and danced around the trees thinking
about all the fun we'd have!

And then my dream came true! "I think it's time for you to spread your wings and see the world," Mom said. "How would you like to see England?"

England! Oh, how I longed to see that faraway country I had read so much about. Would I meet the Queen? I would get to speak English!

There were more people in London than I had ever seen in my entire life, and to my great surprise, no one laughed at me when I told them my name! They even called it pretty and not unusual at all.

"Tonight I will show you something special," Mom said, and we got all dressed up to go to the theater. The theater looked like the most magnificent house I had ever seen. There were lots of people in fancy dresses, and gold chandeliers everywhere.

Our red velvet seats creaked when we sat down.
The stage was mysteriously hidden with a
heavy-looking curtain.

All of a sudden the lights dimmed. The curtain opened and the show began. I felt like lightning struck me! As I listened and watched the story unfold onstage, the people in the audience laughed and cheered. I saw the actors turning into their characters and making us believe in them, and I realized these would be my powers, too!

I would tell stories and make people laugh and dream.

I couldn't wait to tell Mom about my plans, and when I did, she hugged me and said, "Off you go then, my love. I can't wait to watch you tell your stories."

And so I did. I practiced telling stories by acting them out. The more I told my stories, the more confident I got.

I even learned to speak French and went to Paris so I could tell my stories there!

The meaning of my name was right after all.

And so when I found out I was expecting my very own baby,
I thought long and hard about what to call her ... until I
found a name that came from the sky, and from the forest.

Nova Tennessee

Nova, for the star that brings light on the darkest nights, for the promise of a new beginning that each day holds.

And Tennessee, for the beautiful Smoky Mountains
where her father and I waited for her to arrive,
wondering what she would be like.

Now, every day, Nova Tennessee grows and changes.
I can't wait to watch her learn to use her powers.

What about you?
Do you know the meaning of your name?
And have you found your own special powers yet?

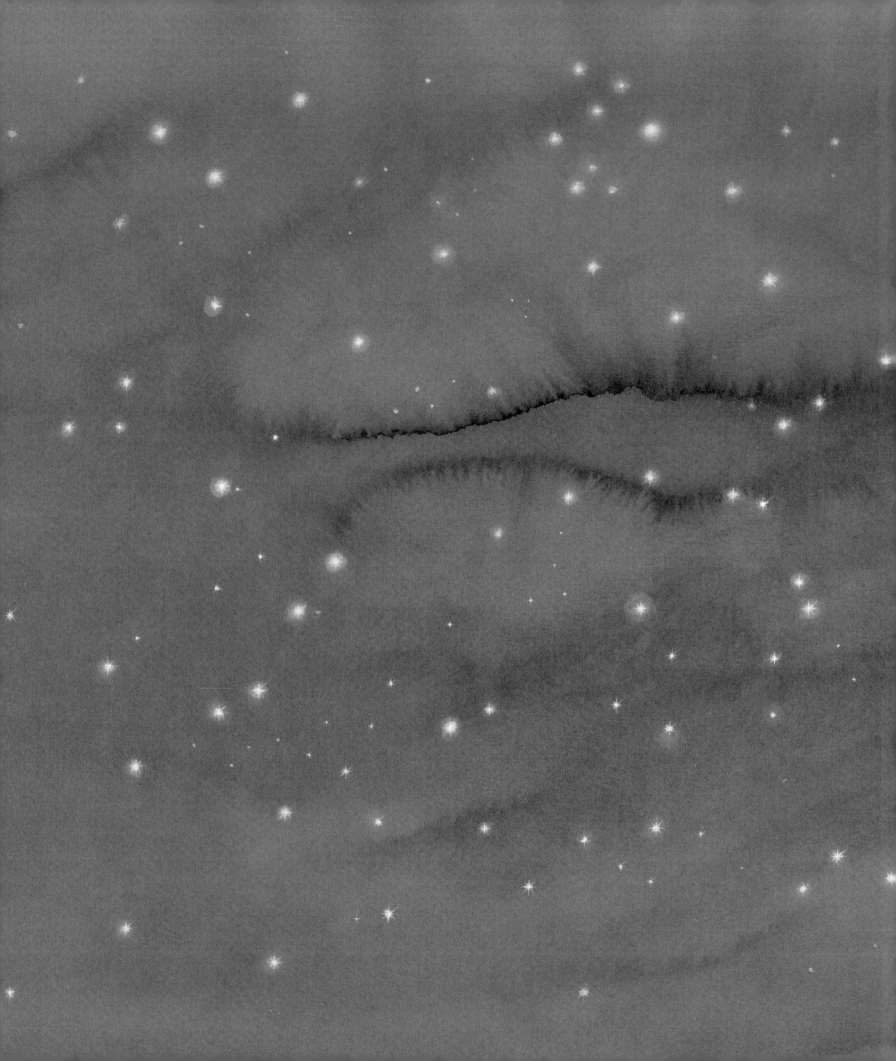